AN APPROACH TO SANITY

CEN

AN APPROACH TO SANITY

A Study of East-West Relations

BY

FIELD-MARSHAL THE VISCOUNT

MONTGOMERY

OF ALAMEIN, K.G.

COLLINS
ST JAMES'S PLACE, LONDON
1959

Contents

Introduction

IN MAY this year, 1959, I was the Chichele Lecturer at Oxford University, giving two lectures. The title for the lectures was 'The conflict between East and West'.

Each lecture was broadcast the same evening in the Third Programme of the B.B.C., and later was broadcast to the Russian people in the overseas programme.

I have received many requests that the lectures be published in book form. It seemed to me that, if this was done, certain articles written by me in the *Sunday Times* since I withdrew from active employment in NATO should also be published—since they have a general bearing on the whole subject of the conflict.

On the 4th April 1959 we celebrated the tenth anniversary of the signature of the instrument setting up the North Atlantic Treaty Organisation. An article by me, entitled 'NATO—Past, Present and Future' appeared in the *Sunday Times* on the 29th March 1959. Since NATO has played a foremost part in preserving peace during the post-war years, this article is a natural starting point.

Mr. Macmillan had visited Moscow the month before, in February. His visit was the beginning of a new personal relationship between the statesmen of East and West; it opened up possibilities of relaxing the tension between them. But it would need to be followed up. And this was arranged, it being announced later that the Foreign Ministers of Britain, the U.S.A., France and Russia would meet in Geneva on the 11th May 1959.

I then decided that I would visit Moscow myself, and meet Mr. Khrushchev. I wanted to have a talk with the Soviet leader and clear my own mind on certain aspects of the problem. So I went to Moscow on the 28th April 1959 and returned to London on the 1st May. The articles in the *Sunday Times* of the 10th and 17th May contain the account of my talks with Mr. Khrushchev and his military advisers.

On the 20th June 1959 the Foreign Ministers dispersed for a breathing space, having argued the toss for six weeks without making any progress. They were to meet again on the 13th July. I wrote an article in the *Sunday Times* of the 12th July entitled 'Brass Tacks at Geneva' in which I endeavoured to define clearly and simply the issue on which any progress must depend.

The Foreign Ministers finally dispersed on the 5th August 1959, no agreement whatever having been reached. But before they parted it was announced that President Eisenhower had invited Mr. Khrushchev to visit the U.S.A. in September and that he himself would visit Russia later in the year.

It seemed to me that at long last some sanity was now to be introduced into international affairs. Once the leaders of the two most powerful nations concerned in the conflict had agreed to meet and discuss ways and means of solving the points at issue, then surely we should see an easing of the strain—at any rate in Europe.

That is what I hope and believe will happen. And if it does, and if we then move forward to better and more peaceful days, do not let us forget that the man who inaugurated this personal contact between the great leaders was Mr. Macmillan—who had the courage to visit Moscow and talk with the Soviet leader, in spite of black looks from certain of our allies who thus showed a great lack of imagination.

The newspaper articles I have mentioned, and the two Chichele lectures, are now brought together in this small volume in order to place on permanent record my thinking during a very momentous period in our history. I am indebted to the *Sunday Times* for permission to re-publish the articles concerned.

I will conclude this introduction to the approach to sanity by quoting the last verse of Shelley's *Hellas*, which seems to me to fit the present times exactly:

> *Oh cease! must hate and death return?*
> *Cease! must men kill and die?*
> *Cease! drain not to its dregs the urn*
> *Of bitter prophecy.*
> *The world is weary of the past,*
> *Oh, might it die or rest at last!*

Montgomery of Alamein

F.M.

Isington Mill,
Alton, Hampshire
November 1959

I

NATO—PAST, PRESENT
AND FUTURE

*I relinquished my appointment as Deputy Supreme Allied Com-
mander, Europe, on the 20th September 1958, and withdrew
from active employment in the British Army—after fifty years of
continuous and unbroken service. I had had ten years experience
of international relationships in the realm of defence, during
which time I had been in frequent touch with the political leaders
of the nations of the free world—and with the leaders of certain
other nations not so free.*

*And so I reckoned I knew a good deal about Western defence
and possibly more than anybody else, since I had been actively
engaged in it, in responsible positions, for ten years. I joined the
Western Union Defence Organisation in October 1948. And
then on the 2nd April 1951 I joined up with General Eisenhower
in the NATO military organisation, and remained in it for a
further seven years.*

*On the tenth anniversary of NATO I decided to write the
following article.*

ON THE 4TH APRIL 1949 the North Atlantic Treaty was
signed in Washington by the Foreign Ministers of the
twelve Powers which were the original members. Greece

and Turkey joined the Alliance on the 18th February 1952, and Federal Germany on the 9th May 1955. The total of nations in the organisation then became, and remains today, fifteen.

It is worth while to cast back in history and clear our minds about the origins of NATO. By May 1945 we had won the German war militarily, but had lost it politically *vis-à-vis* Russia. The United States and Britain then withdrew the greater part of their armed forces from the continent of Europe. In the case of Britain, the people were exhausted after the war and the soldiers wanted to get home. We also ran down our armaments programme and turned over industry to the art of reconstruction. The Soviet Union did not follow suit. They maintained their forces in Europe on a war footing and kept up their armament production.

As time went on it proved impossible to reach agreement about the four-Power control of Germany and the drafting of peace treaties with ex-enemy States. The climax was reached at the end of 1947 when the Soviet representatives walked out of the Allied Control Council in Berlin. Thus was let down the Iron Curtain which split Europe, indeed the world, in twain. In the face of all these troubles there was, in fact, nothing to stop Russian forces from overrunning Western Europe, if they ever wished to do so—except possibly the possession by America of the atom bomb.

It was Sir Winston Churchill who, in a speech at Fulton, Missouri, in March 1946, first put forward the idea of a defensive alliance by peace-loving nations. At the time the idea was rather frowned on. But it was taken up in September 1947 by Mr. St. Laurent, then Foreign Secretary of Canada, who, in an address to the General Assembly of the United Nations, expressed concern at the complete inability of the Security Council to ensure protection to the free world. He added that the nations should seek safety for themselves by joining in an association of States willing to accept specific obligations in return for greater security. He was soon to be proved right.

It was that great man Ernest Bevin who then conceived the idea of a Union in Western Europe, which would be backed by the United States and the British Dominions. This led to the formation of the Western Union, which was brought into being by the Treaty of Brussels—signed on the 17th March 1948, by Belgium, the Netherlands, Luxembourg, France, and the United Kingdom.

Again the next move came from Mr. St. Laurent. On the 28th April 1948, he put forward publicly in the Canadian House of Commons the idea of a single mutual defence system which would include and supersede the Brussels treaty system and be designed to bring in the United States and Canada and certain other nations, in order that the Atlantic Ocean could be made secure for getting help to Europe. This idea was brought to fruition by the formation of NATO. It is often forgotten that the defensive alliances of the West, up to and including NATO, were conceived in Canada. An exception would be the Treaty of Dunkirk in March 1947, between France and Britain; but this was aimed expressly against renewed German aggression and has no further validity today.

Let it be said at once, and without any qualification, that NATO was faced with a difficult task—and it has succeeded. Its contribution to the security of the free world has been tremendous. There are two other regional organisations, the Baghdad Pact and the South-East Asia Treaty Organisation. But NATO is by far the most important. Indeed, in my view, only by increasing the effectiveness of NATO by all possible means will we find the real answer to the political and military problems of the freedom-loving nations of the world.

The NATO treaty was born of collective insecurity, and much of the energies of the member nations have been directed primarily to strengthening their defence against aggression. But to provide an effective defence within the limits of financial possibilities and economic realities demanded *collective* defence in the true sense of the word—and this has never been possible because each nation wanted self-sufficiency.

What, then, is the situation in NATO today? It has achieved its object in preventing war. It now needs a thorough overhaul and a comprehensive review of its political and military structure to meet the changed conditions. There is a tremendous waste of money and effort, and a great deal of unnecessary duplication.

The global aspect of the political and military problems of the free world is almost completely disregarded. NATO has looked inwards at its own problems and has neglected to study what has been going on elsewhere. A member of the NATO Council said recently that a single NATO policy towards what is going on in the world outside NATO is not possible—nor is it desirable. It seems unnecessary to comment on this amazing statement!

There is not even a common policy *within* NATO. How can you have a common defence without a common policy? In recent days we have seen two conflicting statements—one by the President of the United States that no more ground forces are needed in Europe, and one by the Supreme Allied Commander in Europe that he wants more soldiers!

Quite recently, France has intimated that her Mediterranean Fleet will be withdrawn from NATO command and will be under national control in war. This seems to have created quite a storm. General de Gaulle has presumably been studying the naval command set-up in the Mediterranean and can make neither head nor tail of it. Nor can I! Indeed, the whole command structure in NATO needs revision. If we embarked on war with the present command organisation, the result would be disastrous.

Then again, it is high time the NATO authorities realised that complete integration of national forces into a NATO force is not the answer. The plan for a European Army proposed by the French Prime Minister, M. Pleven, in 1950, hit that rock and foundered. What is needed in NATO is national forces, balanced collectively, and welded into a fighting machine by the closest co-operation. The operative word is 'co-operation'—not integration.

Surely we look at NATO problems through the wrong end of the telescope?

We had a scare over Berlin in 1948, and now another one is on the horizon. Of course we must stand firm against all scares and threats. But what is the point of discussing the status of Berlin except within the concept of the future of Germany *as a whole*? We must stand firm on this issue and continue to insist on our rights in Berlin until the whole problem is sorted out. And surely it is illogical to try to solve the *German* problem without first solving the *European* security problem. The greater contains the less—and not *vice versa*. And over all is another paradox— to work on the assumption that the East German Government doesn't exist. It does exist.

A much more flexible attitude is needed in our approach to these problems. For instance, how much longer can the NATO nations continue to keep their forces in other people's countries? As the security problem stands today the only thing I would fear would be the Russian Army. I would like to see it back in Russia, 1,000 miles away. Why not let all national forces return to their own countries? This certainly cannot be done yet, and, in any case, not until the European security problem is solved. But at least we could begin to discuss it, and to negotiate, and both sides to show good faith by beginning to thin out in certain geographical areas.

Such action involves no question of so-called 'disengagement'. The forces of Federal Germany could well guard the NATO front in Central Europe—and who better? And why should not a United Nations set-up lend a hand in Berlin and other places? Anyhow, the operative word is 'negotiate'—not threaten. This is where I think Mr. Macmillan is so sensible.

I never can understand Americans who say that if their forces left Germany they would leave Europe. Why? I thought we all belonged to an Alliance, pledged to support any or all who are attacked or are in danger. If the needs of the Alliance demand that an American Corps of, say, two divisions should be located in France, which they would, I presume it would be kept there. Similarly for a British Corps of, say, one division and Corps troops—about 20,000 men.

And if Russia in return demanded that an equal number of Russian troops be kept in, say, Poland or some other satellite country, I can see no objection.

Once we can get the European security problem settled, all these things become possible. And then the present enormous defence budgets can be drastically reduced—for the benefit of all concerned, including Russia. And we could then begin to co-exist peacefully in Europe—or at least try to, which does not happen at present.

Generally, in NATO it takes far too long to get any of these things done because of the interminable arguments about unimportant details which go on in the committees of the NATO Council—of which there are a large number, too many in fact. There is too much arguing and too little decision. A much simpler organisation is needed.

The two basic needs in NATO are unity and leadership.

The fact is, too many of us are allies only in name. We are a group of nations unable to agree how we get where we want to go. It is ridiculous to suppose that we can be allied to the north of a certain parallel and, at the same time, pursue our contradictory national policies to the south of the same line. Yet this is what we do—and have done ever since the late war ended in 1945. If we could establish true unity in NATO we would be well on our way to solving all our troubles. But it must be a unity of purpose—not of mechanism. Without such unity, the result of the conflict between East and West may well be in some doubt.

Then comes the need for leadership. This is particularly difficult in a group of democracies since you cannot give orders but have to persuade. After the late war the leadership of the free world passed to the United States. But American leadership has been intermittent in its pulsation, for all sorts of reasons. On the other hand, the East, if tactically agile, has certainly been systematic.

I reckon the time has come for a change.

Britain must now come forward and supply the consistency, acting as a sort of moral broker. We can't go it alone. And the difficulty is to make the rest of the free world go it together; that is where our brokerage should come in, as Mr. Macmillan is at present showing—and very well too.

It is unfortunate that we are always having to cork up colonial leaks, e.g., Kenya, Malta, Cyprus, and now Central Africa. This takes our eye off the ball; also, however unjustifiably, it gives scope to those Americans who adopt an attitude of holier-than-thou anti-colonialism; and even more unjustifiably it makes it easier for the Russians to portray us to colonial peoples as old-fashioned exploiters. The crux of the whole matter is this. We admit at once that the achievements of NATO have been terrific. We have stopped a major war in Europe, nor will there be one in any foreseeable future so long as NATO is strong in unity and leadership. We have learnt to work alongside each other. And, all too slowly, some—but not all—are beginning to realise that we must look outwards if we are to win the next round of the contest between East and West—and not just inwards at ourselves. But if we are to do this effectively, we must have an agreed policy which links NATO with the world outside NATO—and this we have not got.

If NATO is to survive and become the vigorous and healthy organisation we all desire, there must be changes. The first requirement is a thorough review of the whole organisation. Those who drafted the Treaty obviously had this in mind. Article 12 reads as follows:

> After the Treaty has been in force for ten years, or at any time thereafter, the Parties shall, if any of them so requests, consult together for the purpose of reviewing the Treaty, having regard for the factors then affecting peace and security in the North Atlantic Area. . . .

Well, the Treaty *has* been in force for ten years. Here then is the authority for reviewing the whole organisation, and in particular the military structure. A major trouble is that, the Standing Group being in Washington and the Permanent Council being in Paris, the Council tends to get its military advice from the Supreme Commander at SHAPE—which is altogether wrong. It should come from the Military Committee of NATO, composed of the Chiefs of Staff of the NATO countries. This unsound method of working has tended to make the Supreme Commander the most powerful personality in the organisation, whereas the Secretary-General should have this position.

The review I have suggested would take all these matters into close consideration. But it would have to be carried out by a very small committee under a very strong chairman. And none of them should be serving in the NATO organisation today; unless this happened, nothing would happen.

The greatest danger facing NATO today is complacency; perhaps apathy is a better word. It has often seemed to me that NATO is becoming a sort of mutual-congratulation society, thinking all is well and refusing to face facts. After a successful battle, the good general is he who looks over his army, examining where things need improvement, where the organisation is cumbersome, where the command structure failed, where changes would be desirable, where there was waste and inefficiency—and so on. NATO should now do the same.

It has won a successful battle. This, then, is the time for review and overhaul of the whole organisation, in order to progress.

Change is inevitable. Progress is not inevitable. Progress depends on courage to face the facts, and then to make sound decisions based on those facts. Only if it acts in this way, can NATO go forward with confidence into the future.

Published in the Sunday Times
on 29th March 1959

2

MY TALKS WITH MR. KHRUSHCHEV
IN MOSCOW

In February 1959 Mr. Macmillan had visited Moscow.

The next month, in March, it was announced that the Foreign Ministers of Britain, the U.S.A., France and Russia would meet in Geneva on the 11th May 1959. I decided to visit Moscow before the meeting of the Foreign Ministers. I went as a private citizen, without any authority except my own.

There were three things I particularly wanted to find out:

1. *What was the Russian view on war, an all-out nuclear war? Were they prepared to risk such a war to gain their ends, or were they not?*

2. *What did the Russians think about the Germans? Were they frightened of them—or not?*

3. *What did the Russians think about the Chinese? This was an important point in my thinking. An interesting situation would arise if it emerged that the Russians were afraid of what might happen on their two flanks—a united Germany in the West, and hostile China in the East.*

The two articles which now follow give the account of my talks in the Kremlin with Mr. Khrushchev.

I

THE CONFLICT between East and West is a vast subject and historians will place its origins far back in history. My own practical connection with the conflict is limited to the period since the end of the Second World War. In the years immediately after the end of that war we were badly placed and we lost ground everywhere. Then we got ourselves organised in Europe, by means of NATO, and we lost no more ground there, though there are, of course, grave dangers elsewhere—notably in Africa, and in Asia, which includes the Middle East.

The situation today in Europe is that after years of toil and frustrations the Western Alliance has worked itself into a good position *vis-à-vis* the Eastern bloc, led by Russia. On no account must we weaken our position. On the contrary we must hold it, and continue to strengthen it by unity of purpose among the Western nations. Our aim is peace—peace with honour, and not by appeasement of the other side. But we must be willing to negotiate towards a reduction of the present tension, wherever and whenever this can safely be done without jeopardising Western unity, and Western security and interests. What is the good of continuing to hurl threats of nuclear destruction at each other? That way leads to war, with all the misery which war brings to the mass of the people.

We want to bring our children up to be good citizens in a peaceful world. We must not hand over to them the unsolved problems of today, with all the disunity, suspicion and mistrust which exists. But as things are, they hear continual talk of war—and it is not good for them.

A major trouble on our side is that when some sensible ideas for easing tension are put forward, such as those recently suggested by Mr. Macmillan, they are immediately submerged in a morass of allied discussions, and finally only some compromise skeleton emerges. This lack of common purpose, and interminable argument about unimportant detail which tends to cloud the real issue, suits the Eastern book very well. It is a sign of our lack of true unity.

An all-out nuclear war between East and West is not wanted by either side. The new key to strategy, the nuclear deterrent, has helped in this respect. But there are a very great number of problems to be solved. If the solutions to all these problems are put into one 'package' deal, it will not be possible to reach agreement on the package. A great deal of suspicion and mistrust on both sides has first got to be removed. Surely we must begin slowly, agree minor moves which do not affect the military security of either side, and advance step by step—creating mutual confidence as we go?

Having considered the matter carefully, I finally decided I would like to visit Moscow and discuss the tangled problem of European security with the Soviet leader and his military advisers. For me it would be a personal and private fact-finding visit, to investigate the problem for myself, and to see if there was any light at the end of the dark tunnel—and I was certain there must be some light, as surely as the dawn follows the night.

And so, having first ascertained from Mr. Macmillan that such a visit by me would cause no embarrassment to him or to the British Government, I wrote to the Soviet Ambassador in London and the matter was quickly arranged.

One point was firmly fixed in my mind. If it became clear that there was no light to be seen at the end of the dark tunnel, no gleam of hope, we in the West must not be afraid of what might come. We would have to brace ourselves and put no limit on our endurance—knowing that if war came it would be a nuclear war. The nation which puts a limit to its fight to preserve its own way of life, will abandon the struggle when that limit is reached—and will inevitably succumb. Never let us do that!

Such were the thoughts which had formed in my mind when the Russian jet TU–104 in which I was travelling landed safely at Vnukovo Airport, some twenty miles outside Moscow. But how to put all these things over to Mr. Khrushchev? And what answers would I get?

It was dark. But powerful arc lights lit up the scene and I at once recognised my old friend Marshal Sokolovsky, surrounded by a milling crowd of Press correspondents and photographers. It was a most friendly welcome. After some difficulty we managed to get to our car and depart for the British Embassy. My first engagement was to visit Mr. Khrushchev the next morning, the 29th April, in the

Kremlin. I went alone. In addition to the Soviet leader the following were present at the meeting—Marshal Sokolovsky, an interpreter, and an official from the Soviet Foreign Office. I sat alone, faced across the table by four Russians. I asked the Soviet leader if he would give me his views on the present situation in Europe; he said he would gladly do so. This is what he told me:

The overall aim of the Soviet Union is peace. The simplest way to achieve this aim is to dissolve the two military blocs, NATO and the Warsaw Pact, and withdraw national forces back to their own countries. But this is not agreed by the Western Powers. A disturbing factor is that nuclear weapons are now assuming a paramount role and this creates a nervous attitude throughout Europe—and indeed the world.

We have reached the position where each side, East and West, could devastate the other with nuclear weapons. It was commonly thought that Russia could not devastate the United States; this was very false thinking; Russia could most certainly devastate the United States with her missiles.

But all such talk led only to mistrust and suspicion. And the greater the degree of control by one side over the employment of missiles, and defence against bombers, the greater the mistrust on the other side.

Some steps must be taken to do away with this situation. We must find a formula which would be agreed by both sides. The simplest way was to make a Peace Treaty with the two Germanys, the Federal Republic and the German Democratic Republic—with real guarantees for West Berlin. If the Western Powers refused to do this, then Russia will act alone and negotiate a Peace Treaty with the Democratic Republic; if this should lead to war, Russia cannot escape her destiny.

Nobody wants to see the re-unification of Germany at present, but few people have the courage to say so. Adenauer doesn't want it. The French don't want it, nor do the British. Russia certainly doesn't want it.

He asked me for my views on this subject. I said it was my personal opinion that the re-unification of Germany, though very desirable, was, today, not practical politics—because of what he had said.

He continued:

If it could be agreed that national forces should return to their own countries, then Russia would accept a very comprehensive plan of inspection and control of national territories. But a truly comprehensive inspection system is not possible so long as the armed forces of the two blocs are facing each other in Europe, ready to be alerted for battle at short notice. To allow inspection of each other's forces and dispositions under such conditions would be absurd. But once all the forces have been withdrawn to their own countries, the proper conditions for inspection would be created; the war situation would then be calmed down, and an inspection system would gradually remove mistrust and produce confidence.

Here I interposed a question. I said he gave me the impression that Russia was afraid of Germany, and of the revival of that country. Would he care to enlarge on this point?

He said Russia was 'apprehensive' about Germany—not afraid—and about a possible revengeful spirit which might arise in that country. It looked as if Federal Germany might soon take a leading position in Western Europe; she might eventually persuade the Western Allies to march eastwards. I said I couldn't believe that would ever happen. He then said the day might come when a united Germany would again march westwards. I said I also didn't believe that would happen, and if by chance it did, I hoped the Russians would lend a hand to stop it.

I then asked if Russia was frightened of what China might do—in the long run. He said 'No'. China was a 'hinterland' for Russia. They were two nations 'back to back', each looking after the other's rear areas.

At this stage he asked me to comment on his remarks.

I said it was clear from what he had said that there was a very tangled situation to be sorted out. That was a matter for the political leaders of both sides. I was a soldier. I had taken part in two world wars, both of which could, in my opinion, have been prevented by the political leaders of those days. In neither case had we received the benefits which it was hoped, and even promised, peace would bring. It must not be allowed to happen all over again, with the suffering and misery war brings to the mass of the people of a nation. We must plan to hand over a more peaceful world to the youth of our nations.

It would be a mistake to try and solve all the problems in one 'package' deal; it is doubtful if there would ever be agreement by all concerned on the package. Surely we should start slowly, take one point at a time, and gradually remove suspicion and mistrust as we go along?

A situation existed in Europe which *could* lead to all-out nuclear war between East and West. The so-called 'cold war' was not my business. But if the cold war led to a hot war, we should all have failed—politicians and soldiers. The first thing for us all to do was so to negotiate that any possibility of a hot war will be quickly removed.

The immediate danger spot appeared to me to be in Berlin; there was a situation there which, if not quickly solved, could lead to a hot war—and this I gathered from what he had just said. Let us therefore settle that quickly. We could ease the present tension by agreeing two measures:

First: get the United Nations Organisation 'in' on the Berlin problem. The aim would be to produce a sound United Nations plan for West Berlin, with definite United Nations guarantees, acceptable to both sides.

Second: to agree a simple inspection plan, possibly in a defined area initially, which could be extended gradually as mutual confidence was gained.

These two measures would begin to remove suspicion and mistrust. Once that desirable state of affairs had been reached, all the other points he mentioned in his analysis could be discussed between political leaders in a far better atmosphere than was possible today.

Mr. Khrushchev said he agreed with these two measures, and would be prepared to discuss how they could best be implemented.

We then dispersed. Mr. Khrushchev agreed we should meet again the next morning, 30th April. I spent the afternoon touring the streets of Moscow in order to see the people. And I visited a large Department Store for children and bought some toys for my grandchildren. The Russians wanted to take me to the theatre that night. But I declined, saying that I wanted to be quiet and think about the problem which confronted us.

We met again in the Kremlin at 11 a.m., and again I faced the same four Russians across the table. This time I opened the discussion myself, with Mr. Khrushchev's agreement. I said I had spent the previous afternoon in the streets of Moscow, seeing the Russian people shopping before the May festival. I had visited the great University on the hill outside the city, with its 22,000 students. I had visited a children's Department Store. It is these people who suffer if war comes—the ordinary people, the common man, the man in the street, the children. Let both blocs, East and West, co-operate to extinguish all the sparks which could possibly light a fire which might result in World War III.

But so great was the suspicion and the mistrust on both sides, it would be useless for the two blocs to discuss major problems until some of the suspicion and mistrust had been removed, and a calmer atmosphere prevailed. I was alarmed by one statement he had made yesterday—that if the West would not agree to peace treaties with the two Germanys, then Russia would negotiate a peace treaty with East Germany, even if this should lead in the end to war. I hoped he did not mean that. No good could follow from trying to 'go it alone'. Let us take one thing at a time, and move forward step by step, creating a calmer atmosphere as we go. The West certainly would not flinch if it all ended in war. But nobody wanted it to end like that. That way led to devastation, and to misery for all the peoples on both sides, East and West. Although I accepted his statement that he wanted peace, he might not get the peace he needed if he continued to 'push us about' so much. Let us negotiate, and cease to irritate each other.

So far as Germany was concerned, there were two troubled situations, two sparks which could light a fire—West Berlin, and German peace treaties. He (Mr. Khrushchev) wished to solve them both at the same time. I suggested that a better plan would be to separate the two problems. First solve the West Berlin situation, and thus produce confidence throughout the Western Alliance— postponing the peace treaty proposals indefinitely until all concerned were satisfied about the Berlin situation. This might take some time; but what did that matter? What *would* matter was if undue haste brought on a major war. We must not let that happen.

Mr. Khrushchev asked how I saw the United Nations handling the Berlin problem. I said that was not my business, but he pressed for my opinion. I then suggested that the matter should be handed over to the Secretary General to investigate, and to produce a plan acceptable to both sides. A United Nations force consisting of neutral nations might be introduced gradually into West Berlin, and the forces of the western nations could possibly be scaled down at some later date, as mutual confidence developed. But any United Nations plan must be acceptable to both blocs, East and West, with firm guarantees for the West Berliners.

Mr. Khrushchev said he, personally, agreed with my views. He admitted he had previously wanted to solve the two German situations at the same time. But he now saw the force of my remarks. In view of what I had said, he was prepared to separate the two problems, tackling the West Berlin problem first and postponing the peace treaty problem for the time being. He would agree to that procedure.

He asked me about the inspection plan I had advocated. I said it should not be hurried. Keep it simple. Begin with a small defined area in the middle of Europe and gradually extend it as mutual confidence is restored. Inspection teams must be truly international. The plan, if sound and practical, could well begin at any time. It would all help to remove suspicion and restore confidence. But don't try and force an Eastern plan down the Western throats too quickly. Go quietly at it, and evolve a simple plan acceptable to both sides. Mr. Khrushchev said he agreed in principle with what I had said.

All in all, it seemed to me when I left Moscow that something had been achieved. Mr. Khrushchev had agreed to separate the two immediately troublesome problems in Germany, to tackle West Berlin first, and to postpone indefinitely the peace treaty proposals. He had shown a willingness to be flexible in his approach to the whole business and to eliminate all hot war possibilities as a first priority. I was myself convinced that neither he, nor the Soviet Marshals, really wanted to achieve their aims by war—a hot war.

So far, so good. But no doubt some hard bargaining lay ahead! I will conclude this article by saying that I was received by the Soviet leader, and by the Soviet high military authorities, with the greatest kindness and courtesy. Our talks, though very frank, were conducted in a most friendly atmosphere. I formed the opinion that Mr. Khrushchev is a most able person—indeed, I would describe him as brilliant.

For my part, I have established a friendly contact with the Soviet leader. And I have received a warm invitation to visit Russia whenever I like—either for further talks or for a holiday.

In the next article I will give some impressions of Moscow and its people. And I will endeavour to assess the possibility of creating such a situation, such a lessening of tension, that East and West can 'live and let live' for a generation ahead—which would surely be for the benefit of all mankind.

II

MOSCOW IS a vastly different city from when I paid my first visit there in January 1947. In those days the whole Russian nation was recovering from the trials and tribulations of Hitler's war. The destruction caused by the German invasion of 1941, and by the subsequent fighting, was very evident. The people were poorly clad. Food was scarce. Housing conditions were appalling, and that problem seemed almost impossible of solution. On my return to London from the visit in 1947, I informed the British Government that it would be fifteen to twenty years before Russia would be in a position to fight a major war with any chance of success—if, indeed, she ever wished to embark on such a course, which I doubted. Those were the days of the Stalin regime, and the people looked depressed, and frightened.

Today all that has changed. The Stalin regime has passed away. Food seems to be plentiful. The children look well and happy. The housing problem has been tackled energetically and great blocks of flats have sprung up in the main cities. The secret police do not operate as before; there seemed to be more freedom for everybody, and less fear. And the people generally are much better dressed; by that I mean that the quality of the clothing looked far better than formerly.

The Soviet leader, Mr. Khrushchev, is a very remarkable person. He has a quick and clear brain and you never have to say anything to him twice. Furthermore, he is a realist. He sticks to the point all the time. He has an amazing knowledge of the facts of any subject you raise, and is never at a loss for his answer. In fact, one gets the impression that he is very well briefed by his staff, or else he gets on terms with all the problems himself. His office table was a delight to me; there were no files or papers, and all was neat and tidy!

It is difficult to describe his face. He has an infinity of expressions, which change rapidly. The Almighty fashioned us humans in clay. I reckon a modern sculptor would find it difficult to make a good bust of Mr. Khrushchev in sculpture!

He is without doubt a brilliant political leader, with all the arguments at his finger tips. You would have to get up very early in the morning to get the better of him in discussion.

The Marshals of the Soviet Union whom I met had all fought through both world wars. Marshal Malinovsky, the Soviet Minister of Defence, had served as a soldier in the ranks on the western front in France in the First World War, and had often come in contact with British troops. He told me that the English soldiers had taught him several expressions which they said he would find useful in France. He could only now remember two, and caused great amusement by repeating them at a lunch given in my honour at the Red Army Officers' Club in Moscow. One was 'Kiss me'. I won't mention the other one; it is quite unprintable!

It was delightful to meet again my old friend Marshal

Sokolovsky. We got to know each other well when he was Chief of Staff to Marshal Zhukov in Berlin in 1945. He is an Hon. KBE and asked me if I could send him some ribbon of the Order of the British Empire for his new tunic—which I did immediately on my return to London. He is now Chief of the General Staff of the Armed Forces of the Soviet Union.

It is often thought that the Russians are planning to attack the West the moment a favourable opportunity occurs. I do not believe this for one moment. They may use the 'threat' of armed action, indeed of war, to gain their political aims—no more. But if ever a nation today wanted peace it is Russia, in order to build up her economic strength and to raise the present low standard of living of the people. They have nothing to gain from a nuclear war; indeed, they have everything to lose.

But they think *we* want war, and will attack them when we are ready. I assured them this is not the case.

Furthermore, I pointed out that, like them, we have nothing to gain from a nuclear war. The West will never attack the East. Our strength is for defence, in case they attack us. It is difficult to make them believe this, so great is the suspicion and mistrust. And it is made all the harder by statements from our side about what we could do to Russia with our nuclear weapons.

It's a curious situation. Two blocs, East and West, each thinking the other intends to attack them at any moment! And the plain truth is that neither side has any intention of attacking the other. I refer, of course, to an all-out shooting war, a nuclear war. And the amount of money each side spends on preparing to repel attack is stupendous. It would be interesting to know if such a situation has ever existed before in history. It is almost Gilbertian!

I often recall the last verse of the poem by Robert Southey, 'After Blenheim', which runs as follows:

> 'And everybody praised the Duke
> Who this great fight did win.'
> 'But what good came of it, at last?'
> Quoth little Peterkin:—
> 'Why that I cannot tell' said he,
> 'But 'twas a famous victory.'

The operative line is the third.

The trouble is, the West spends such vast sums in preparing for an all-out nuclear war which is unlikely to take place, that nations cannot provide sufficient resources for scientific experiment and development, and for the cold war—which is actually in progress, which is, of course, our main problem, and on the winning of which everything depends.

A further trouble is that to compete successfully in the cold war, the West must look outwards, and not just inwards at its own affairs—and it is not very good at this.

Although an all-out nuclear war in Europe is remote, there are grave dangers elsewhere—notably in Africa, and in Asia (which includes the Middle East). It is in those areas that the cold war will be fought—a battle with economic and political weapons, and not military ones. And to lose ground in Africa and Asia will tend to weaken our position in Europe.

In all these matters the Western Alliance must see the whole 'wood', and not just fix its gaze on certain trees. The whole wood is the world. The cold war is a global contest.

We now come to the 64,000-dollar question; or perhaps there are two questions.

1. Is it possible, given time, that the Russians can become part of Christendom? Many will say it is not possible. For myself, I am not so sure.
2. Is it possible to create such a situation, such a slackening of tension, that for a generation ahead we and the Russians can 'live and let live'?

Perhaps we had better try and answer No. 2 first. If, indeed, it is possible to live and let live with the Russians for a generation—say twenty-five years—then No. 1 surely comes within the field of vision—however remote it may seem at present.

Anyhow, it would be criminal not to try. We must not slam the door against any possibility of peaceful co-existence with the Russian people, if it can be brought about with honour to both sides.

Well, I believe the answer to No. 2 could be 'Yes'. But we will have to change our tactics. We must cease to hurl threats of destruction at the Eastern bloc. We must cease to be boastful of our nuclear strength, and what we can do with it. Bellicose speeches by Service Chiefs will do no good.

And the East will have to change its tactics too—in the same manner.

Instead, let us visit each other.

Let the Chief of the Imperial General Staff visit Moscow, and see the Russian Military colleges. Let us invite the Russian Service Chiefs to visit Britain.

Let us try to be friendly, like I did. It is not an expensive journey. My ticket for the round trip cost £142 4s. od. The Government would get a good dividend from such a small expenditure; I certainly did myself.

And the more trade we can do with the Russians, the better; that is a very good way to get on friendly terms with them.

The Russian people like the British. I sensed that very quickly. Any friendly gesture by us could well open the door to improved relations between East and West as a whole.

The cold war will, of course, continue; that is very clear. And it will be a long contest. But in an atmosphere of 'live and let live' for a generation ahead, the cold war might well become less turbulent. Who knows?

Hitherto the West has worked on the assumption that it is not really possible to resolve the present deadlock with the Eastern bloc, and that it may well end in a nuclear war —for which we must prepare. But are we quite sure about this? Is there a gleam of hope anywhere? If so, let us look for it, and, having found it, exploit it.

Neither side wants a nuclear war.

> *'But what good came of it, at last?'*
> *Quoth little Peterkin.*

And if we can find a gleam of hope, and we exploit it, and we find the right answer to No. 2 question—the answer we would all like to find—then surely No. 1 question becomes a possibility? And then we could hand over a peaceful world to our children's children.

I'm all for trying.

Published in the Sunday Times
on 10th and 17th May 1959

THE CHICHELE LECTURES

ON

The Conflict
Between East and West

DELIVERED IN OXFORD

ON THE 15TH AND 22ND MAY 1959

I had agreed in 1958 to give these lectures, and much of my time during the winter of 1958–1959 was spent in preparing them.

I decided to make the first lecture historical, but only insofar as it was known to me. For this lecture I had to carry out certain research and the book in which I found most of what I needed was one written by Herbert Feis, a distinguished American, entitled Churchill, Roosevelt, Stalin: The war they waged and the peace they sought.

This is a magnificent study and I would recommend it to anybody who wishes the best information on that subject.

In the second lecture I dealt with the post-war years, from 1945 up to the present time.

The two lectures together constitute one balanced whole and should be read as such. My general conclusions will be found at the end of the second lecture.

The reader should note that the first lecture was delivered four days after the Foreign Ministers gathered at Geneva (which was on the 11th May 1959). The second lecture, on the 22nd May, came when the Foreign Ministers had been talking for nearly two weeks—with no result.

3

FIRST LECTURE

The Story up to the end of the Second World War—May 1945

THIS IS a vast subject and I imagine that historians will place the origins of the conflict at least as far back as the Battle of Marathon. But you gentlemen will know far more about that than I do. My best contribution to your thinking will be to confine myself to events in the military and political field of which I have some knowledge, in the hope that this may fill in gaps in your own study of the subject.

In this first lecture I will deal with the past, but only insofar as it is known to me. That will take us from the time of the First World War up to and including Hitler's war. You may think that this period is no longer as interesting as the period of the post-war troubles which now encompass the world. That may be true. But we must have some general background for our study.

Then in the second lecture we will examine how the conflict grew and developed during the post-war years, and try to discover why things in the world today *are* as they are. And to conclude, I will see if there is anything I can suggest which will provide a reasonable basis of thought and action in the dilemma in which we in this country, and indeed we of the West generally, find ourselves.

If we are to plan the future wisely we must learn from the past. As Maeterlinck said:

the past is of use to me as the eve of tomorrow;
my soul wrestles with the future

Let us take a brief glance at the past. What has happened to our nation during the past forty-five years?

Twice during this period we have taken part in a world war. In the first one, the Kaiser's war, our Empire casualties included one million dead. We won the war but we made a sad mess of the peace. You will remember that the war propaganda took the line that it was a 'war to end war'.

The period after the war was one of great hankering after peace. It was also a period when there was a serious loss of belief in religious and moral principles, and a swing towards materialism as being the best way to achieve prosperity.

In any case we did *not* achieve prosperity, and during much of the nineteen-twenties and nineteen-thirties there was heavy unemployment.

What is more, we did not achieve peace. Some twenty years after the end of the Kaiser's war, we became engaged in a second world war (Hitler's war)—and that before we had really recovered from the first.

But worse was to come.

As a nation we were totally unprepared for the Second World War in 1939. However, in 1940 the grim realities of what we were fighting for were forced home to us and we rose to the occasion—as the British always do in the end.

But when after some four years of Hitler's war it became clear that in co-operation with our Russian and American Allies we were going to win, again we lost sight of realities. The Grand Alliance of nations began to break up, and the true intentions of Stalin began to disclose themselves. Later, after the war had ended, intense nationalism began to develop in areas which in the past were passive or subordinate, and the world began to drift towards the turbulence in which we find ourselves today. And to crown it all, once fear had disappeared, disunity began to appear in the Western ranks, thus making it more difficult than ever to hold our own against a centrally-controlled Communist East.

Overall then, in modern times we have had two major wars, both of them probably brought on by unpreparedness, and, after each of them, a total failure to achieve the benefits which it was hoped and even promised that victory would bring.

It is against this general background that I propose to examine the conflict.

Since Russia, with her doctrine of international Communism, is the root cause of all our troubles here in the West today, we should now cast back and see if we can discover when her motives began to create suspicion in Western circles.

When the growth of Fascism in Germany and Italy began to cause alarm in the West, and the possibility of war loomed ahead, conversations took place regarding collective action to restrain Hitler and Mussolini. The Russians professed a wish to take part in these talks. But Russian overtures were not accepted with any great eagerness; their motives were mistrusted. And it would seem rightly so, because in August 1939 came the non-aggression pact between Russia and Germany. The ink had hardly time to dry on the pact before Stalin began to show his hand. He swallowed the three Baltic States (Estonia, Latvia, Lithuania), the eastern part of Poland, a portion of Finland, Bessarabia, Bucovina, and certain islands on the Danube.

All these seizures of territory by Stalin took place when Russia was in association with Germany. Possibly they alarmed Hitler. Anyhow, the association was always an uneasy one and on the 22nd June 1941, Germany attacked Russia. This gave us a powerful ally. But Churchill, while gladly welcoming Russia as an ally, soon noted with some concern, if not surprise, that Stalin seemed to be at least as interested in post-war frontiers and spheres of influence as in prosecuting the war.

Stalin thought he could hold the German onslaught until the bitter Russian winter set in. The spring of 1942 would be a critical time but he considered that America would by then be in the war—after which final victory would be certain.

Two months after Russia had been invaded, that is in August 1941, Roosevelt and Churchill had met in

Newfoundland and had signed the Atlantic Charter. This pledged the signatories to acquire no new territory, and to oppose any territorial changes not agreeable to the peoples concerned. When the United States entered the war (7th December 1941) its Government proposed a Declaration of United Nations, binding all the governments at war with the Axis in an all-embracing war alliance, and, also, pledging them to support the principles of the Atlantic Charter. This was subscribed to by Soviet Russia and was signed on the 1st January 1942, in New York. Here at once were the seeds of discord. Despite their signature of the Declaration, it was very clear that the Russians were going to insist on territorial claims which could not be reconciled with the principles of the Atlantic Charter and the United Nations Declaration.

Both Roosevelt and Churchill were well aware of this attitude on the part of Stalin. Indeed, they had known about it in June 1941 when they had decided to act in support of Russia. As the United States were not yet in the war, their support could only be by way of material supplies, and, in view of the straits we were in, our aid would also have to take this form. Neither Roosevelt nor Churchill were disposed to bring into discussion Stalin's ambiguous position, or indeed to enter into unprofitable arguments which might cause the Russian war effort to slacken.

As the German assault against Russia became intensified and more difficult to hold, so Stalin became the more dissatisfied with the British war effort in the struggle against

Germany and Italy. And he took no apparent interest in the Japanese threat in the Far East, which threat was causing Churchill considerable anxiety. Early in September 1941, even before the Americans came into the war, he made his first demand for a second land front to be opened in Europe by the British before the end of 1941—one which would draw thirty to forty German divisions away from the Russian front. After the American entry into the war, this demand was to be repeated over and over again, and the question of 'when' such a second land front could be opened was one which at times threatened to shake the Alliance to its foundations.

With the Japanese attack on Pearl Harbour on the 7th December 1941, America entered the war against both Germany and Japan. But all attempts to persuade Stalin to declare war on Japan met with a firm refusal.

The United States Chiefs of Staff had always reckoned that sooner or later Japan would take some action which would bring America into the war. Even so, realising that, they had come to the view that when that time came the defeat of Germany must be the primary objective.

But we now see (December 1941) Churchill becoming alarmed that the American people might fail to see the war as a whole, and might pursue the war against Japan in the Far East, leaving Britain to fight alone against Germany and Italy in Western Europe, in Africa, and in the Middle East.

There were indeed strong impulses tending to pull the American forces towards a major war effort in the Pacific.

Against this, Stalin was urging the immediate opening of a second land front in Europe.

However at the first great British-United States war conference in Washington in January 1942, it was agreed that we defeat Germany first while containing Japan.

Notwithstanding this clear agreement, we read in a book by an American historian that 'an effort of growing size and impetus was maintained in the Pacific'.

Also that 'the flow of troops and equipment to the Far East went on; until August 1942, at least, it was actually greater than across the Atlantic'.

This distribution of American military power was at times to cause alarm to the British Chiefs of Staff—and as a result, occasionally, mistrust.

We now come to a major point of thinking in the American military organisation which was to have a far-reaching effect on the conduct of the war.

The Americans, once in the war, considered that all military actions must be based on purely military grounds and need not take into account their political repercussions. This thinking led to a postponement, for military reasons, of decisions about political issues. The eventual result was to leave the field of political action open to manœuvre within the Alliance—with the risk, indeed gradual growth, of suspicion. It was also a temptation for each member of the Alliance to use its military strategy to pursue its own political aims. And it can be put forward with a certain justification that each, in fact, did so—in some degree— Russia fastening her grip on the continent of Europe,

Britain always anxious about her position in the Mediterranean and about her life line to the Far East through the Suez Canal, while the United States looked longingly to the Pacific theatre.

This militarily unsound thinking—and remember I speak to you as a soldier—was to have serious results as the war progressed and, in my opinion, is responsible for certain of our troubles today.

During 1942 two events of major importance tended to cause rifts in the Alliance.

The first one was the proposed Treaty between Russia and Britain. Stalin wished to have the Soviet frontiers dealt with in the Treaty. Churchill was inclined to agree. He thought that the gravity of the war situation demanded that Russia should keep the frontiers she occupied when attacked by Germany in June 1941. Stalin was very steamed up on this issue, and Churchill reckoned that if Stalin was not given in the Treaty the frontiers he demanded, it might affect the Russian war effort.

Roosevelt was entirely opposed to any discussion of frontier problems until the fighting was over. He tried to lure Russia away from her insistence on the immediate discussion of post-war frontiers by promising quick military relief—the opening of a second front in 1942, which was of course not possible so far as Western Europe was concerned. In the end the Treaty of Alliance between Britain and Russia was signed on the 26th May 1942, all provisions regarding territories and post-war frontiers being omitted. Stalin had given way on the strength of what he no doubt regarded as a promise of a second front *in Europe* in 1942.

The second event of major importance was the argument which developed between the Americans and the British about where the second front should be—whether it should take place across the Channel in 1942, or in 1943, or whether the Allied forces should land in North Africa in 1942 and exploit the situation in the Mediterranean first.

On this issue there was a tremendous difference of opinion and contest of wills.

Early in 1942 the planners in Washington, who included General Eisenhower, prepared plans for the cross-Channel operation in 1942. A limited beachhead was to be seized in France in 1942 (Operation Sledgehammer). In 1943 was to come the breakout from this bridgehead (Operation Roundup) and the all-out 'drive' to Berlin to defeat Germany.

Up to this time the Americans had never fought the Germans in the second war and they had no conception of what a formidable enemy they were.

In my opinion the American plan for the cross-Channel invasion of France in 1942 would have involved the Allies in a disaster which would have prolonged the war for years. The Americans wished to meet the giant German strength, and smash it in a decisive effort before all else—and then turn all their own great strength against the treacherous Japanese. The British wished to postpone the stern encounter until the German strength had been worn down by continual bombing, her Italian ally had been knocked out of the war, and she was threatened from the Mediterranean side. The knock-out blow would then be delivered, following an invasion of Normandy.

To my mind, the British strategy was the sounder of the two.

Anyhow, the British rejected the American plan for a cross-Channel operation in 1942. The conquest of North Africa and Sicily, and the invasion of Italy, followed.

The Quebec Conference in August 1943 agreed the cross-Channel invasion of Western Europe for May 1944. The Russians were not represented at Quebec and therefore this decision had to be conveyed to Stalin—no easy task. The operation had been first half-promised to Molotov for 1942 by both Roosevelt and Churchill, then hinted at for 1943 at the Casablanca Conference in January 1943, and in August 1943 definitely postponed until 1944.

I suggest that, even at the risk of some repetition, before proceeding further in our study we ought to take a quick look at the relationship which had grown up during the war between Churchill, Roosevelt, and Stalin.

It always seemed to me that the Americans never realised that the British Empire had fought alone for nearly two years against the combined might of the Axis Powers, before the United States ever entered the war. The British people bore unaided the full weight of the contest in its initial stages, and suffered accordingly.

Other nations had either been struck down or looked on at the conflict from the touch line.

Roosevelt worked hard to get the United States into the

war, with only limited success. It is not easy to unify the great American nation on a specific issue. It was the Japanese who finally did it for him; their action at Pearl Harbour unified the Americans in a few minutes.

The great aim of the American Chiefs of Staff then was to concentrate all available forces for a cross-Channel invasion of France, and to smash Germany by a decisive blow in 1942—only six months after they had entered the war—so that they could then turn their great strength against Japan.

Churchill and the British Chiefs of Staff knew better. And they were right. When the American Army went into battle for the first time in the European theatre in North Africa in November 1942, one year after they had entered the war, the troops were found to be very 'green'. Churchill and his military advisers knew they could never be sufficiently 'battle-worthy' to play their part in Europe against the full might of the German Army in 1942, or even in the summer of 1943.

This became a major cause of argument. And, of course, Stalin backed the American view; he wanted a second land front in Western Europe in 1941 if possible, and certainly in 1942. He did not mind how many Americans were killed. We did. So the controversy at times rocked the whole Alliance.

Stalin was always inclined to underestimate the British war effort before Russia came into the war. Otherwise he would not have called for a second land front in Europe in 1941. He told me in 1947 that he never had any doubts about the final defeat of Germany once the United States entered the war. It is therefore easy to understand that his main preoccupation was to grab as much territory as possible on his western frontier before Russia became engaged in the war (which he reckoned was bound to happen in the end), and to fasten his grip still further on eastern Europe once victory became certain.

Roosevelt and Churchill were both fully alive to this. Roosevelt reckoned all questions of frontiers could be handled at the peace conference when the fighting stopped. Churchill knew better; but he wasn't prepared to embark on arguments about frontiers if such arguments were likely to cause Russia to 'let up' on her war effort. The British military situation in 1941 and the early days of 1942 was desperate, and he wanted the maximum effort from the Russians.

It is interesting to note how Roosevelt and Churchill each tried to woo Stalin in his own way. Each often wanted a good talk with Stalin alone. Each was somewhat suspicious of the other seeing Stalin alone!

So in this trio of war leaders, each a giant in his own nation, and each a determined personality, there was bound to be friction and disagreement. Overall, the trumps were held by Stalin—and the other two knew it.

Let us now turn to January 1943, the time of the Casablanca Conference, at which the momentous decision was taken to impose unconditional surrender on Germany. Stalin did not attend the conference; the decision was taken by Roosevelt and Churchill and communicated to Stalin,

who of course agreed since it suited his plans to the letter—
as we shall see.

It is commonly thought that Roosevelt's announcement
at a Press conference at Casablanca on the 24th January 1943
that the Allies would impose unconditional surrender on
Germany, Italy, and Japan, was made on a sudden impulse
and that he had not thought about it earlier. This is not the
case.

In the spring of 1942 a committee in Washington had
been studying 'end of war' problems, and had been
impressed by the situation at the end of the Kaiser's war
when there had been an armistice only, and Germany had
not been required to submit unconditionally. This faulty
decision had been, they reckoned, directly responsible for
the Second World War. The committee recommended
this time the imposition of unconditional surrender.

It was never made clear what was meant by the statement. Did it mean that Governments were to surrender
their whole nations? And would there be Governments,
anyway? Or was it to be merely the unconditional surrender of the armed forces?

Anyhow, Roosevelt had been considering the problem
for some time in his own mind. And when he announced
it at the Press Conference, Churchill spoke in agreement.

I have often wondered whether Roosevelt had realised
the full political repercussions of the decision he announced.
It must mean that the Germans would fight to the last;
that the British and American forces would meet the
Russians in the middle of Germany; and that there would

then be no German Government to deal with. In that event, unconditional surrender by whom?

It is very plain to me that at this time Churchill was deeply concerned with the many political problems which must arise as the British, American and Russian forces moved on, and finally met in the middle of Europe. He had wanted to take his Foreign Secretary (Eden) with him to Casablanca, but Roosevelt asked that there should be no Foreign Office or State Department representatives present. Against his own better judgement Churchill had agreed.

The Casablanca Conference was held at a most important time. The end of the war in Africa was in sight; the Germans were in difficulties on the Russian front; plans were being made to knock Italy out of the war.

In fact the final victory of the Allies was now certain. It was merely a question of 'when' that would be. Tremendous political issues were going to arise during 1943, particularly in Italy. And as the Russian forces moved westwards, the Balkan States would once again come into the political arena.

If Foreign Secretaries had been present at Casablanca, I find it hard to believe that all these vital issues would have been disregarded. At any rate the pros and cons would have been fully discussed before the decisions were taken.

Nations go to war for political reasons. When it is clear you are going to win, political decisions become paramount; it is then essential so to direct the operations that you end the war with a political balance favourable to win the peace. The Clausewitz doctrine that war follows peace, operates also in reverse—peace follows war.

Understanding what must follow from the decision of unconditional surrender, and knowing that great troubles lay ahead with Stalin over eastern Europe and the future of Germany, the Western allies should surely have ensured that their forces gained possession of the great political centres of Central Europe before the Russians—notably Berlin, Prague, Vienna. If this had been laid down as the object by Roosevelt and Churchill in January 1943, in my considered view as a soldier, we could have grabbed all three in 1944 before the Russians.

But it was not laid down. And it may well be that Roosevelt and his military advisers would not have agreed; they reckoned all political issues should be left for discussion till the fighting was over. First win, then argue. I reckon you should decide what you want to win; then maybe you needn't argue, anyway. It must, of course, be remembered that the European Advisory Committee had, during 1944, worked out zones of occupation for the Allied forces in Germany when the war ended. The Russians naturally wanted the western border of their zone to be as far west as they could get it, and in the committee they had agreed with the British a western boundary substantially the same as their present zone. The Americans didn't seem to bother much about it; indeed Roosevelt initially didn't want the United States to have a zone at all, and intended to get the American forces back to the U.S.A. as soon as possible after the defeat of Germany.

It is interesting to note how, at this period, neither the British nor the Americans seemed in any way upset at having the Russian Army as far west in Germany as had been agreed in the plan put forward by the E.A.C.

Roosevelt reckoned that by patience and friendliness the Russians could be guided to our way of thinking and that he (Roosevelt) could bring this about. He liked to assume the role of a mediator between the British and Russians when the argument became heated—as for instance over Poland.

But Churchill's thinking was very different. Before the Yalta Conference (February 1945) we find Churchill telling Roosevelt that 'the end of the war may well prove to be more disappointing than was the last'.

Then during the Conference itself the atmosphere was friendly and it seemed that the Russians might well become reasonable partners in the post-war years. But this feeling of trust gave way to suspicion very soon after the Yalta Conference ended—when Stalin began to take the necessary steps to ensure that the whole of eastern and central Europe would be ruled by Governments under the control of Moscow.

Even the American Government was now disturbed. Churchill was, of course, deeply distressed. He had failed to get the American Government to understand that 'Soviet Russia had become a mortal danger to the free world'.

He has since written in *Triumph and Tragedy*, page 456:

'Thus this climax of apparently measureless success was to me a most unhappy time. I moved amid cheering crowds, or sat at a table adorned with congratulations and blessings from every part of the Grand Alliance, with an aching heart and a mind oppressed with forebodings.'

How right he was! And how right on this score he had been all through! And so, as the German war was being won we see the gradual loosening of the Alliance. And then, when the war was over, Stalin was able to resume his revolutionary aims of world domination by the onward march of international Communism, and this finally broke the Alliance.

Could it all have been avoided? Historians will argue the toss for many years and will find the subject a happy hunting ground.

Let us consider British-American relations first. I reckon history will record that Roosevelt and his advisers were generally suspicious of Churchill's motives. A celebrated American, who was sent by Truman as a special envoy to see Churchill in May 1945, is said to have reported as follows:

'The Prime Minister is a very great man but there is no doubt that he is "first, last, and all the time" a great Englishman. I could not escape the impression that he was basically more concerned over preserving England's position in Europe than in preserving Peace. In any event, he had convinced himself that by serving England he was serving Peace.'

The Chairman of the American Joint Chiefs of Staff is

reported to have made the following comment on this statement:

> 'This was consistent with our staff estimate of Churchill's attitude throughout the war.'

I disagree with these expressions of opinion. My own personal relationship with Winston Churchill finds no evidence to support such statements. The authors seem to forget that if Britain had not stood firm in 1940 under her great leader, when all seemed lost, the situation in the United States today would be vastly different. They forget that America declined to take part in the fight for Freedom until she herself was directly attacked. By standing firm when all seemed lost, the British people, under Churchill, saved Western civilisation.

I have always considered that while the break-up of the Alliance into East v. West could hardly have been prevented, the Western nations could have ended the war with their forces further to the east than actually happened. They would then have been in a better position to achieve a political balance in Europe more favourable to themselves than that which has actually emerged. And Berlin might well have been included in the Western zones. As it was, when the British and American forces met the Russians in the middle of Germany, they had to withdraw a considerable distance to their own zones because they could not go back on their pledged word about zonal boundaries given at Yalta.

But to achieve the desired end, political considerations

would have had to be given their proper place in the planning once it was clear we were going to win the war. Knowing the troubles which lay ahead with the Russians, the Western nations should have ensured that they would be well placed politically *vis-à-vis* the Russians when the fighting stopped.

To achieve success in these respects, the proper decisions would have had to be taken early in 1943—in fact immediately after the Casablanca Conference in January 1943.

The final conference between the Big Three took place at Yalta in February 1945. The bargaining power of the British and Americans at that conference was not very great. The early days of 1945 saw the Western front reeling from a terrific German blow in the Ardennes. That battle in the Ardennes caused the Western Allies to lose six weeks in time with all that entailed in political consequences for post-war Europe.

A study of the Yalta Conference will reveal that while the three leaders parted with expressions of eternal friendship, agreement on the more urgent problems of post-war Europe was not reached. Final victory began to come closer soon after the Conference broke up; but as it came closer, arguments over the vital issues became more inflammatory. Stalin remained suspicious of American and British attempts to maintain spheres of influence in the Balkans, or any other areas near the Russian frontiers. It was clear to all that Stalin was not going to hold to the vows he seemed to have made 'when the going was bad'.

15th May 1959

4

SECOND LECTURE

The Post-War Years

IN THIS second lecture I propose to discuss the situation which obtained at the end of the German war in May 1945, and then follow the sequence of events up to the present times.

In May 1945 we had to pay for losing the war politically —although we had won it militarily. It is a dismal story, as will appear.

The act of 'unconditional surrender' was signed by the German High Command. It was, in fact, a military surrender and not one of submission by the German Government of Admiral Doenitz—which after Hitler's death in Berlin claimed to represent the German nation and which was later arrested by the Allies.

Indeed, the Allies did not recognise any German Government *which could* surrender.

Here was a pretty pickle!

This was a very different situation from that which had been envisaged by Churchill, Roosevelt and Stalin. They had agreed that a Control Council would be set up in Berlin which would dictate to a central German Government how the country was to be run.

But there was no central German Government. This suited Stalin very well. He refused even to discuss Control Council problems until the British and American Governments had withdrawn their forces back within the zonal boundaries which had been agreed at the Yalta Conference. This meant giving up to the Russians very large areas of Germany which the British and American forces had overrun before the fighting ceased. But past agreements had made this inevitable. And Stalin gradually fastened his grip very firmly on the whole Russian Zone of Germany—now known as the German Democratic Republic.

Then was let down the iron curtain, which split Europe, indeed the world, in twain. The conflict between East and West had begun in earnest.

Our problems in the British Zone were terrific.

Over one and a half million unwounded German fighting men had surrendered to the British Group of Armies at Lüneburg Heath on the 5th May. One million German wounded were in hospital, with virtually no medical supplies. Over one million civilian refugees had fled into the British area before the advancing Russians. There was little food available in the area. Transport and communication services had ceased to function; industry and agriculture were largely at a standstill.

There were some twenty million Germans in the British Zone. The destruction caused by bombing to their homes, and to living accommodation generally, was very great. The civilian population was generally in a state of abject misery.

It was essential to get normal life going again and to arrange for this vast number of Germans to be fed and housed. If this was not done before the winter set in, famine and disease would run riot through the British Zone—indeed through all the Western zones as a whole—and that would prove a most serious embarrassment to the Western Allies.

I found myself in charge of all these affairs.

I kept the German Military Command in operation in my area and, through it, controlled all the German prisoners of war. These were demobilised by categories (farmers, miners, electricians, carpenters, civil servants, etc. etc.) and sent back to their homes to resume their civilian trades—in plain clothes, of course, or in uniform without buttons, and as quickly as could be arranged by the British and German staffs.

In order to re-establish civil government, I disposed my Corps and Divisions in such a way that military boundaries coincided with the civil boundaries akin to our county councils, boroughs, rural district councils, and so on. The task of the Army in its various echelons of command was to assist local civil authorities, burgomasters, etc., to get local government working smoothly. We then appointed Regional Commissioners. And the whole organisation worked up to the Headquarters of the C.-in-C. and Military Governor—myself.

The system worked, which was the great thing. And the Germans obeyed.

Meanwhile, we had got the Control Council constituted

in Berlin. Our troubles with the Russians began soon after its first meeting on the 30th July 1945. It quickly became apparent that Stalin had no intention of carrying out the plans for the future of Germany which had been agreed at the Potsdam Conference.

Early in October 1945 the London Conference of Foreign Ministers ended in disagreement. The conference had been assembled to work out peace treaties with ex-enemy states—as had been agreed at Potsdam.

It was now clear to me that we were heading for trouble in a big way. So I went over to London later that month (October 1945) and told the Prime Minister (Attlee) that Four-Power control of Germany could never be made to work. I added that the Western Powers must now prepare for a continuous struggle with the Communist East—which would last for a long time. This prophecy at least, made in October 1945, would seem to have come true!

Meanwhile the countries of Western Europe had begun to drift apart, the fear of the German military machine being no longer present. But later, certain nations began to get anxious about the threat from the East. The cold war began to intensify and a number of treaties were made as the beginning of collective security in Europe.

The Brussels Treaty was signed on the 17th March 1948; this brought the Western Union into being.

Meanwhile General Marshall had made his famous speech about economic aid for Europe and this was legalised in the U.S.A. on the 3rd April 1948. But Stalin refused Marshall Aid for Russia and for her satellite countries—although some of the latter had begun by welcoming it. This was a clear indication that Stalin did not want Europe to recover economically; he preferred a disrupted and dismembered Europe; recovery might have impeded the spread of Communism.

The Russian blockade of West Berlin which began in June 1948 served to show the Western nations something of the troubles which lay ahead; it was finally defeated by the tremendous feat of the air lift.

This blockade created great tension in the Western world, and considerable alarm, and it was decided to create a, Western Union Defence Organisation which would prepare plans for combined action in case of attack—which it was thought might very well come.

This defence organisation came into full operation in October 1948.

Finally the North Atlantic Treaty Organisation was brought into being, known for short as NATO—the Treaty being signed on the 4th April 1949. The next step was for the Western Union military organisation to be absorbed into NATO—and this took place in 1951.

Finally, on the 2nd April 1951, General Eisenhower assumed operational control of the military forces of the defensive alliance. I joined him as his Deputy.

The task in NATO was to build up political, economic and military strength in the North Atlantic area in order to be able to stand firm against the onward march of international Communism.

This proved to be difficult. If a group of nations want to

co-operate closely in defence matters, they must first decide their political association in some detail. This had not been done. We very soon found that no nation was willing to make any sacrifice of sovereignty for the common task. Intense nationalism developed as soon as fear began to disappear—which it did when the Western Union defence organisation was absorbed into NATO and the American forces in Europe became part of the defensive organisation.

But we soon found that if armed forces were to be organised within the limits of financial possibilities, joint defence within the alliance would be necessary. But each nation wanted everything. It was not understood, and it is not even today, that if every nation wants self-sufficiency there is little value to be got from the alliance.

However, we carried on somehow, but under difficulties.

Our task initially, was to build up military strength in order to *defeat* an attack, which it was thought the Russians might conceivably launch while the West was weak militarily. However the attack did not materialise, and in due course the progress of science gave us nuclear weapons in ever-increasing quantities. This gave us the power to destroy to an extent never before visualised. That power could be developed into such a powerful offensive weapon that it was clear that no profit from war could come to any nation. An aggressor nation might inflict tremendous damage on Western civilisation but would itself suffer equal or even greater damage.

Thus was born the new key to military strategy, the nuclear deterrent. This is an offensive nuclear capability which can be launched by aircraft and missiles from air, sea and land, and which, provided it is suitably dispersed, cannot all be knocked out or neutralised by a surprise attack.

Both the West and the East possess the nuclear deterrent, the means of delivery today being primarily the manned bomber. But we are moving into the missile age and in due course the number of manned bombers will decrease—but not yet, and perhaps never completely.

While we were building up strength in the NATO area to deter attack, what was going on in the rest of the world?

Let us examine the global situation. But before doing so I would remind you that the struggle against international Communism is a world-wide struggle and is not one which can be confined to the NATO area.

I am going to show you that the NATO nations failed to view the problem in this way. And because of their lack of vision, the West is badly placed at the present time in what is essentially a global problem. One could put it another way—while watching every 'tree' in the NATO area, the NATO nations failed to see the global 'wood'.

Here is a map[1] which shows the line-up of nations about the end of the last war—say in August 1945. The Western Allies are shown in green—Russia, Yugoslavia, and Albania in red.

[1]The references to the maps are, of course, to the coloured maps displayed in the lecture room during the original delivery of the lecture.

Some countries are shown in yellow, as not yet committed to the coming cold war struggle.

You will notice that some of the yellow countries are marked with red bars because they were occupied by the Russian Army in 1945—notably Manchuria, North Korea, East Germany, and the Russian satellite countries between the Baltic and the Black Sea.

Now compare this map with the next one, which gives the situation say last year—in 1958.

The 'red bar' countries are now red.

Tibet has disappeared behind the iron curtain.

China has become red, with her population increasing at the rate of about twenty million a year, and possibly more. For the moment China is occupied with her own internal affairs. But if she became closely united with the economic strength of Russia, she would in due course become a menace to the countries of the Pacific and South-East Asia. Mao-Tse Tung will need to be watched.

Now look at South-East Asia and the Indian Ocean.

We see that Indonesia, Indo-China, Burma, Ceylon, India—are all lost for 'cold war' purposes to the Western cause. Here is an area where the Communist cause is making a sustained political and economic effort. It is an area of immense strategical importance to the Western cause—particularly Indonesia and India.

Now see what has happened in the Middle East.

Much of what was green in 1945 has become yellow. The United Arab Republic of Egypt, Syria, and the Yemen is shown as half red—perhaps it should be red. The position of Iraq is not entirely clear at present, though it is not re-assuring. The map shows only too clearly the confusion to our cause brought about in this area by Western disunity, jealousy and short-sightedness. As far as the Western nations are concerned, we want to trade with the nations of the Middle East and to have freedom of movement through the whole area—that is all. You can say, in fact, that the integrity of the whole Middle East is economically and strategically essential to the West.

Now look westwards along the north coast of Africa.

The Sudan and Libya, both formerly green, have become yellow.

There is considerable unrest in what was formerly French North Africa. The French have a real problem in Algeria, which is flanked by the independent States of Tunisia and Morocco—whose position is somewhat obscure.

Overall, a comparison of the two maps shows very clearly how the Communist regime has been creating trouble for the Western world outside the NATO area for many years.

And lastly look at Europe. Here our losses have been great. Eastern Europe, red and yellow in the first map, is now red; it is lost to the Western cause.

Germany is divided.

The Communist tide has advanced to within a day's car drive from Paris.

But there have been gains in Europe. The North Atlantic Alliance has been formed.

Norway, Denmark, Portugal, Greece and Turkey have

taken their place with the other countries of the Western world. Federal Germany has remained steadfast—despite many temptations.

Yugoslavia, red in 1945, is today yellow. Under President Tito she is now a neutral country.

So in our balance sheet, a 'cold war' balance sheet, only Europe shows a profit. And the reason is NATO. In the first few years after the war we lost ground everywhere. Then we got ourselves organised in Europe and we have had no more losses there.

This is not a suitable occasion to assess blame as between individual nations for all these lapses. But, overall, we can say this.

The trouble has been that the NATO nations, some of which are world powers, fixed their eyes on the NATO area and did not bother about what was going on in the rest of the world. In fact, as I have already said, they saw all the trees in the NATO area, but failed to take account of what was going on in the global wood. And they failed to see that the problem was gradually becoming less and less military and more and more ideological and political.

A major problem is that, although we face a global problem, our outlook in NATO has not been global during the past years. The difficulty is that there is in NATO a large group of nations with purely parochial interests which are confined to the NATO area. There is another and smaller group with world-wide interests. It has not been possible to hammer out a common policy between these two groups. Indeed, the World Powers have not even been able to agree a common policy among themselves—one which links NATO to the world outside NATO.

However, we can take comfort from one thing. Because of what has been achieved during the past ten years in building up the economic and military strength of the Western Alliance, NATO Europe is now the area where the military danger is least. The real dangers now lie elsewhere—notably in Asia and Africa.

This is a great achievement, because NATO Europe is probably the most important area in the global struggle; if it were lost, all the rest of the Western world would follow. This great achievement is due to what NATO has done in the past ten years.

The battle of the next ten years will be very different; it will be political, financial and economic. It will be more an ideological war, a battle for the hearts and minds of men, and it will be global—as it has always been in the past. To combat this threat successfully, the West must organise its affairs on a global basis.

The problem can be defined, fundamentally, as follows. Western Europe, including the U.K., is an area on which depends a world-wide economic system. But in that area there is a shortage of raw materials, particularly oil. Also, large quantities of food have to be imported to feed the big populations. The sources of raw materials and food, and the transit areas through which they come to Europe, have to be protected—together with the bases and communications necessary to control them. Failure to do this would lead to the collapse of the whole economic system. The East will strive for success in this direction rather than by resorting to direct military action against the West.

The West, that is the NATO Governments, must understand that they may have to fight a battle anywhere in the world at any time—a battle fought with economic and political weapons, and not military ones.

To what extent has military strength played a part in the contest? Let us have a quick look at this aspect of the problem.

When the war ended in 1945 the cry was 'get the boys home'. Reacting to this popular cry, the British and Americans quickly began to run down their armed forces in Europe. Except possibly France, the other nations of Western Europe hadn't got any armed forces; they had all been occupied by the Germans and their forces disbanded.

The whole emphasis in Western Europe was on economic recovery as the first priority. It must be admitted that many of the nations were in a pretty bad way economically after a prolonged NAZI occupation. But they did not understand that economic strength *by itself* is of no avail against the onward march of international Communism— which is prepared to use the threat of war to gain its ends. The needs of economic and of military strength have got to be properly balanced—and this was not done.

The United States certainly did a great deal, and gave generously in economic aid and military equipment. And she kept her own armed forces in Europe, and they are still there—despite the fact that Roosevelt had said in 1944 that he would have to get the American forces back to the United States as quickly as transportation could be arranged when the German war was over.

Indeed, it can be said without any qualification that during the past fourteen difficult years since the war ended, the United States has been a firm anchor to the NATO ship—a solid rock, poised and balanced behind the nations of the Free World, giving encouragement and also generous help from her vast resources. *It is impossible to express adequately the debt we in Europe owe to the U.S.A.*

So we have, with United States help, arrived at the position where, having worked hard to prevent a third world war—and succeeded—our political leaders must now work for some form of overall regulation of armaments compromising nuclear and conventional forces, with a proper control and inspection system.

This will be difficult, and will take time—much time.

Meanwhile, the megaton nuclear weapon preserves peace—a most curious situation.

I suggest there is a need for a new approach, and for greater flexibility in working out some way in which East and West can co-exist peacefully—or at least can try to do so.

If progress is to be made in this direction, there are certain principles which it seems to me would have to be accepted by both sides. Possibly 'principles' is the wrong word. Perhaps they are 'realistic factors', which could help towards a better understanding.

77

I suggest that the more important of these realistic factors are the following:

First: The East, led by Russia, has no intention of launching a direct all-out nuclear attack on the West.

Second: The West, similarly, will never attack the East—not even to launch a preventive war.

Third: It is illogical to expect Russia to agree that a united Germany armed with nuclear weapons can be integrated into the Western Alliance. In any case, the re-unification of Germany is not practical politics *at present*.

Fourth: It is illogical to try and solve the German problem without first solving the European security problem. The greater contains the less, and not vice versa. It is the same in all planning in war. Agree the grand design, the master plan, in the first instance; then work backwards and fill in the details.

Fifth: It is illogical to work on the assumption that the East German Government doesn't exist. It does exist. And for a satellite of Russia the German Democratic Republic is prosperous.

Sixth: It is illogical to work on the assumption that the true Government of China is in Formosa.

We are now in a position to be able to state what should be the political aim of the West—of the Free World. I suggest it should be two-fold:

First: A united Germany in a free Europe. This cannot be achieved until the European security problem is settled. It is a matter of negotiation between NATO and the Russians. Much will depend on whether the six points I have just outlined are agreed in principle. But at the present time, the re-unification of Germany, though very desirable, is just not practical politics—as I have already said.

Second: To work for a friendly China. This will take time—maybe ten to fifteen years, or even longer. But let us not delay. We should have begun years ago. My sixth point, that it is illogical to work on the assumption that the true Government of China is in Formosa, will be important here.

What is the West to do about all this? Two things are necessary: Unity; Leadership.

UNITY

I put true unity as the great and fundamental need of the Western Alliance. With it, we would be well on the way to solving all our troubles. Without it, the result of the conflict between East and West may well be in some doubt.

Before we talk about international unity, perhaps we should put our own house in order and get national unity. We have had it in two world wars; we conquered ourselves; we became a united nation; we conquered our enemies. The Russians, the war being over, retained in

peace the discipline and common purpose that had carried them through the war. They seem to be doing well, whatever we may think of their methods.

Some think that we could get the unity we seek by denationalising nations and setting up some form of world government. That is a great error; we are not ready for that yet. It was on that rock that the conception of the European Army came to grief. The soldier's allegiance and devotion is to his country. For instance, a Turk will willingly die for Turkey; he will think twice before he dies for say Greece, or Italy, or Norway.

What we must become in the Western Alliance is a group of strong nations. But we want to understand that the true and ultimate strength of a nation lies in the national character, in its people, in their virility, in their willingness to work and win prosperity—knowing that they won't get prosperity by merely voting for it, and that if they won't win it themselves they will have to go without it.

The nations of the group must not merely put their signatures to a declaration of common aims and purposes. That is too easy. Words are cheap; so is ink. Most of the communiqués issued after meetings of the NATO Council are worthless. They could be written before the Council ever meets; indeed, work begins on the draft of the communiqué before the Ministers arrive for the meeting!

Nations must show by their actions that they mean to carry their full share of the load, if necessary being willing to make some sacrifice of sovereignty for the common good of all. It is in this latter respect that we fall short today.

I have been in close touch with the Governments of the Western Alliance for many years; I have yet to meet the Government which would put its full trust and confidence in all the other nations.

I do not myself see how this degree of unity can be obtained without leadership. And at the moment there is no obvious acceptable leader in sight—if by 'leader' we mean someone who is able and willing to give clear and sensible guidance to the whole group, and in whom all the member nations have absolute confidence. Such a man would have to be a political personality, of course.

LEADERSHIP

In dealing with this subject I realise I am on delicate ground. My personal knowledge of leadership is confined to the military sphere, though I have been a keen observer of political leadership.

The two are very different. One commands, whereas the other must persuade. Granted, it is better if the general persuades his soldiers he is right, but fundamentally the difference is this—in the upshot he can command them, giving them orders they must obey.

As a soldier, I have been trained to take direct action down certain well-defined lines. I have had available a military machine which has responded immediately and with precision to my touch.

The political leader in a democracy has to act differently. He is trained in subtlety in debate, in weighing up the conflicting interests of his supporters, and he usually has to compromise. Furthermore, the governmental machine is much less precise and exact than the military, and it is not rapid in action even in highly skilled political hands.

In war if a commander compromises on essentials, he fails.

Another interesting point is that the time factor forces the military commander in the field to adopt the best expedient in the time available, which is usually short. The political leader, on the other hand, is seldom forced to give an immediate decision; indeed he cannot, since he has to consult so many others. He therefore delays in order to find the right and accurate answer, and one which will be politically acceptable to his supporters—and to his Allies.

It might be put in another way.

One, the military leader, seizes time by the forelock and adopts the best expedient. The other, the political leader, procrastinates, in order to ensure that what he does is exactly right and politically acceptable.

I suggest to you that the qualities required by a military leader and by a political leader are, in fact, almost at opposite poles. Only a few men in history have possessed both kinds of qualities and competed successfully in both fields. In the realm of the highest ranks in both categories, there have not been many Service Chiefs who have made good political leaders, nor many political leaders who have made great military chiefs.

There is a further aspect of political leadership which is important. Leadership is possibly easy in an autocracy or tyranny, particularly since modern science provides so many safeguards against the assassination of the autocrat.

But in a universal-franchise democracy, leadership is not so easy. Indeed, it *can* become a poor feeble thing because you can only persuade and cannot give orders.

From my own experience I know well how much easier it is to be a commander-in-chief in the field than to be a successful and effective Chief of the Imperial General Staff working in Whitehall.

I reckon the essential points about leadership are decision and action. The leader must decide, order the action to be taken, and see that it is *taken*. He must show to one and all that he is determined to dominate the events that surround him, and that he can do so with a sure hand.

This is simple in the military sphere. But imagine the situation of a leader in a fifteen-nation alliance of democracies who cannot give decisions; he rather has to persuade an infinity of unharmonious musicians to play in tune!

So you see it is all very difficult. Nonetheless, something has to be done and done quickly.

To be successful in the present situation, the leadership of the Free World must avoid the military aspects of what is commonly called 'brinkmanship'. Instead, the leadership must emphasise the will to negotiate; it must be foremost in the willingness to examine with sincerity all suggestions for easing tension between East and West. It must explore the economic approach. In particular it must work for flexibility in all attempts to find a way to 'live and let live' with the East—led by Russia—avoiding all rigidity of thought, while at the same time ensuring the overall security and vital interests of the Free World.

Conclusion

I went to Moscow on the 28th April 1959 to find out what the East thought about all these things. And I found what I wanted.

I went alone, with no 'package' plan. I didn't sing the Western song. I wanted to hear the Eastern song, and to learn what the Soviet leader had to say. And now, having heard East and West, certain matters are clear to me. Let me tell you how I see it.

The constant din of publicity and propaganda forces a Western leader to be more concerned than ever with justifying his position with his own nation, his political party, and his allies and partners in the Alliance. It follows that he is daily less and less able to suggest proposals likely to be acceptable to the East—because of all the Western propaganda. In view of this, it is practically impossible to draft a plan which will be acceptable to everybody.

There is fear abroad in Europe. The Russians fear the Germans greatly; they will never allow a united Germany until the whole security problem is sorted out. Each side, East and West, is frightened of what the other may do. Each side is suspicious of the other. We don't trust the Russians; they don't trust us. Of course, we have different ideologies and social systems, but we don't seem able to 'live and let live' together. Until some of the fear, and suspicion, and mistrust is removed—we will make no headway.

My training as a soldier has taught me that when you are confronted with a very difficult and very complicated situation, which is bedevilled by a vast number of interrelated factors, very clear thinking is needed—and you must aim at simplicity, and cut out all the unimportant trivialities.

You must seek for the one factor on which ultimate success or failure will depend, and then disentangle that factor from all the others and have a good look at it.

In the conflict between East and West, that one factor is Germany. The problem of Europe is the problem of Germany. But Germany is split in two. German re-unification is very desirable and we all hope it will come. And it will come in due course. But it is not practical politics yet, because the Russians won't have it. It may well be possible later on, when some of the fear, and mistrust, and suspicion has been removed. But not yet.

If, therefore, a plan for German re-unification is included in any 'package' plan put forward by the West, the East will never agree to that package. If, however, German re-unification was put in the cupboard for a while, and other problems were tackled first—I reckon we would progress at once.

Do not forget that the East plan for a Peace Treaty with Germany is just as much a 'package' as the Western plan!

The situation has become so difficult, and so tangled, that we must proceed 'Little by little, and bit by bit', creating confidence at each step forward.

If any chink, or gleam of light, is offered by one side—the other side must grasp it with both hands. Any one

85

problem cannot, of course, be considered in isolation—but in a broad context of what we all desire, which is European security and peace. But if a number of problems are put into one package by either side, we run straight into a stone wall. It is as simple as that. Each side is playing with a package.

And it is no good saying that our proposals are very good—the Russians ought to accept them. They might accept certain things, but *not* German re-unification.

The West might accept certain things, but *not* a Peace Treaty 'package'.

So there is a double stone wall in the middle. 'Package' plans are no good at present. The only way to progress is 'Little by little, and bit by bit'.

What are we to learn from all I have been trying to say to you in these two lectures? I suggest we learn the following.

Hitherto the West has worked on the assumption that it is not possible to resolve the present deadlock with the Eastern bloc, and that it may well end in a nuclear war— for which we must prepare. But are we quite sure about this? Is there a gleam of hope anywhere?

There must, of course, be no question whatever of the West 'letting up' on any vital issues. There must be no question of what is called 'appeasement'. We must not yield our position in West Berlin; the rights and interests of the West Berliners must be protected at all costs.

But, having regard to all these safeguards, surely there is some way in which we can co-exist peacefully with

Russia—in spite of our different ideologies and social systems.

The last Foreign Ministers' Conference, and Summit Conference, was held in Geneva in 1955. There has been no progress of any sort since then. It is a dismal story and unworthy of both sides—East and West. Some say we must learn to live in a world of tension—what is wrong with it? There has been no war! I disagree utterly with such thoughts. Do we want our children and our grand-children to grow up in a world of everlasting tension, with East and West hurling threats of nuclear destruction at each other, and with the threat of nuclear war hanging over the world?

Never!

The solution to the problem will be found in the answer to two questions:

1. Is it possible, given time, that the Russians can become part of Christendom? Many will say it is not pos-sible. For myself, I am not so sure.
2. Is it possible to create such a situation, such a slacken-ing of tension, that for a generation ahead we and the Russians can 'live and let live'?

I think we should try and answer No. 2 question first.

If, indeed, it is possible to find a way to live and let live with the Russians for a generation—say 25 years—then No. 1 question surely comes within the field of vision—however remote it may seem at present. Anyhow it would be criminal not to try. We must not slam the door against any possibility of peaceful co-existence with the Russian people, if it can be brought about *with honour to both sides*.

The cold war will, of course, continue; that is very clear. But in an atmosphere of 'live and let live' for a generation, the cold war might well become less turbulent. Who can say? That is the chink of light, the gleam of hope.

Neither side wants a nuclear war.

This, then, is my conclusion—my general thesis. Let us search for a gleam of light, and having found it—as I believe we can—let us exploit it. We should then find the right *answer* to question No. 2—the answer we would all like to find. And if we are successful we could then hand over a peaceful world to our children's children.

I'm all for trying.

Finally, in all this business one thing is very clear to me— the English-speaking peoples of the world must be solidly united. The preservation of Christian civilisation hangs on such unity.

East and West, north and south, wherever the English tongue is spoken, men must clasp hands and forget all else save that they are brothers of blood and speech—eager and ready to unite and to co-operate, and thus save the Free World from being engulfed by the onward march of international Communism.

22nd May 1959

5

BRASS TACKS
AT GENEVA

The situation now was that the Foreign Ministers had dispersed on the 20th June 1959, no progress having been made in their round-table talks—or was the table square? They were to resume their discussions on the 13th July 1959.

I considered that no progress could ever be made so long as all the Western proposals were contained in a 'package plan' which was linked to an early re-unification of the two Germanys.

I decided to write the following article, which could be read by all concerned, on the 12th July—the day before the discussions were resumed in Geneva.

NOW THAT the Foreign Ministers are about to resume their meetings at Geneva, it will be worth while to take a look at certain matters which will have a bearing on their discussions. We should not be disheartened because no agreements have been reached at previous meetings. In my view there was never any possibility of agreement on essentials at that level. Such agreement can be reached only at a summit conference, and nowhere else. Even *there* agreement will be difficult; but it will be possible if those who shape our destinies can face up to certain facts.

A major trouble is the suspicion and mistrust on both sides. Added to this is the constant din of publicity and propaganda; this is so great that a political leader is forced more and more to justify his own position. This brings peculiar difficulties to a Western leader, since he has to satisfy all his partners in the alliance; he is therefore less and less able to suggest proposals likely to be acceptable to the East, led by Russia.

My personal view is that Mr. Macmillan has been dead right all the time. He went to Moscow and broke down Mr. Khrushchev's resistance to negotiate; he now wants to bring the Soviet leader to the conference table—and rightly so.

Political and military pressure from the East, led by Russia, forced the West to build up military and economic strength quickly after the war. This was done, and the nations of Western Europe recovered far more quickly after Hitler's war than they had done after the Kaiser's war of 1914–18. The reason, of course, was American aid. It is impossible to express adequately what we in Europe owe to the United States for that aid—which was freely given, and is still freely given. As a result, the West is now in a strong position.

The East must understand that we will not 'let up' on that position; we will not be pushed about by unilateral threats and actions; we will not abandon our rights in Berlin, which were agreed by Russia at the Potsdam Conference in July 1945. We will insist that the right of the West Berliners to live in accordance with their own choosing must be effectively maintained.

But we will negotiate, and play our full part in trying to solve the European security problem and to find a way in which we can 'live and let live' with the Russian people.

Though we may think them illogical, we must at least understand the Russian fears about their strategical security. Russia sees a ring of Western bases, with nuclear launching-sites, deployed all round the Communist world. They are, of course, for defence. But Russia thinks they are for attack, and during my stay in Moscow I found it impossible to make her political and military leaders think otherwise.

Russia is disturbed about the constant references to a united Germany. Politically, economically, and geographically the German Democratic Republic (East Germany) is Russia's most important satellite, and she is continually investing capital there. Russia will not relinquish her grip on East Germany under present conditions; she will not agree to a re-unification of Germany except under her own terms—which the West will not accept. In fact, a re-unification of Germany is impossible in the present circumstances, and that fact must be faced by the West.

It is not possible to make any fundamental re-design of the Berlin situation until the European security problem has been untangled and sorted out to the satisfaction of both sides. All that we can do is to work for some improvement of the present arrangements. The European security tangle will present a difficult problem.

THE WEST will not have a neutral Germany.

THE WEST cannot allow a re-unified Germany to be in the Eastern bloc.

THE EAST will not allow a re-unified Germany to be in the Western bloc.

The plain truth is, as I have already said, any re-unification of Germany is not possible at present. Everybody knows this; but nobody will say it for fear of offending the Germans.

But what are the facts about the Germans? The facts are that Europe has never known any durable peace since Bismarck created the German Empire. He became Prime Minister of Prussia in 1862. He then embarked on wars in 1864 in Schleswig-Holstein, in 1866 in Austria, and in 1870 in France. These resulted in a unification of the German States, and in 1871 William I was made Kaiser of the new German Empire.

Then in 1914 we had the Kaiser's war, in which war some 20 million men perished or shed their blood. After it, Winston Churchill wrote in *The World Crisis* the following words:

'*Surely, Germans, for history it is enough.*'

But it wasn't.

In 1939 we had Hitler's war, in which it is estimated that some 40 million men, women and children perished in battle, in concentration camps, in gas chambers, or by starvation. Hitler's war left Germany divided.

Can we wonder why some nations are frightened about any re-unification of the two Germanys?

I suggest we must be quite honest. We must say to the German people that any re-unification of their nation is not possible until the European security problem is sorted out to the satisfaction of East and West, and some organisation is created which provides effective guarantees against disturbance of the peace of the world.

Later, when all are satisfied, we will see what can be done. But it cannot be yet. And the Germans must understand that. After all, basically they are responsible for the present state of affairs.

This problem of a united Germany is so acute that there can be no hope of any agreement with Russia so long as all Western proposals are linked to a plan to re-unify Germany. But if German re-unification is put away in the cupboard for a while, and the West admit openly that it is not possible until the more important problem of European security is settled, then I reckon we could at once make progress with Russia and get some agreement on essentials.

If there is any one particular danger against which we must guard, it is that we should get impatient with the present situation and settle for some quick solution which sacrifices all we have struggled for over the weary years. That we must never do. There can be no quick solution; the causes of the conflict between East and West are too deep-seated for that.

The struggle will be hard and long. But time is on our side—and not the contrary, as so many think. No tyranny has ever lasted. Provided we can find some way to 'live and let live' with the Russian people, the progress of civilisation and education will bring great changes in that nation—and all may well work out right in the end.

Published in the Sunday Times
on 12th July 1959